# Whey Aye, Man!

## *A Salute to the Geordie Dialect*

# Carl Hayward

**with illustrations by Richard Scollins
and Steve Iveson**

COUNTRYSIDE BOOKS
NEWBURY BERKSHIRE

First published 2005
© Carl Hayward 2005
**Reprinted 2007, 2010**

COUNTRYSIDE BOOKS
3 Catherine Road
Newbury, Berkshire

To view our complete range of books,
please visit us at
www.countrysidebooks.co.uk


ISBN 978 185306 942 0

Designed by Peter Davies, Nautilus Design
Produced through MRM Associates Ltd., Reading
Typeset by Techniset Typesetters, Newton-le-Willows
Printed by Cambridge University Press

*All material for the manufacture of this book
was sourced from sustainable forests.*

# CONTENTS

# ACKNOWLEDGEMENTS

I would like to thank the following people, organizations, and companies for their help with the research for this book. Without their input, it would never have been written:

Irv Graham of Toon Ale, Steve Iveson, Edith May Douglas of Low Fell, Norma Newton and John Davies of Birtley, Bill Brown, Michael Scully and last, but not least, my wife, Angela, and children, Ben, Molly, and Ellie, for their patience during the time spent researching and writing this book.

Both publisher and author also acknowledge with gratitude the debt they owe to *Ey Up Mi Duck!* by Richard Scollins and John Titford, first published in 1976. That book was the inspiration for the series of regional dialect volumes of which this is one.

# FOREWORD

**W**hy write a book about the Geordie dialect? Well, aal tells yiz why! Approximately three years ago I was looking for a card for me Mam – yes, *Mam* not *Mum* or *Mother*, but *Mam*. Well, it was disappointing to find that there were no real Geordie cards to be had.

Proud to be a Geordie, I thought it was time to give the people of the region the choice they deserved and I embarked upon producing Geordie style cards. My cards depict family life. I have deliberately chosen situations which are typical of families everywhere but have given them a distinctive Geordie flavour. Overleaf are four of my most popular card sketches: Mutha, Fatha, young lad and young lass.

As a result, my interest in the Geordie dialect evolved, and, in the summer of 2004, when Nicholas Battle of Countryside Books approached me, I jumped at the opportunity to write about my interest.

So here it is – the finished article – a book not just about the Geordie dialect, but also about the Geordie way of life. It takes a light-hearted look at the Geordie people, their history and traditions, the area in which they live and their distinctive culture.

My research has allowed me to learn so much about my region and along the way I have talked to some very interesting characters. On both accounts I could have missed out! How lucky I am to have been asked to write this book and how grateful I am that there were no Mam cards to be found in the shops three years ago!

Lads and lasses alike, aa hope yiz aal enjoy read'n' it.

Carl Hayward

# MEET THE GEORDIES

# INTRODUCTION

One of the most distinctive features of the North-East is its well-known dialect. A person who originates from the North-East is easily heard amongst a crowd. A visitor to the region will always be warmly welcomed, and it is often said that people who inhabit these 'nether' regions are amongst the friendliest in the country – or at least people who live here say so!

The dialects of the North-East can be categorized into five broad areas: the 'macam' dialect of Wearside; the 'even further North' (if there is such thing) accent of Northumberland and the dialects of Durham and Teeside respectively; and last, but not least the native tongue of Tyneside, the Geordie dialect.

There has been much debate about regional dialects and a senior lecturer at Reading University has recently talked about 'dialect levelling', which is essentially a process whereby dialects from different regions begin to merge into one another and,

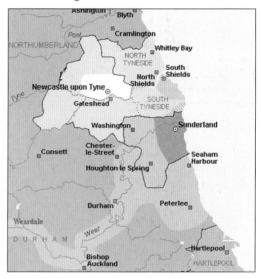

*The North-East.*

in effect, 'even out'. It is fair to say that some of the Geordie words used by older generations may not now be used by the younger of us, but nevertheless there still exists a very distinctive dialect in the North-East.

It is important to note at this point that a typical Geordie does, in fact, come from England, not Scotland, contrary to some opinions. Also, most Geordies, I think, will agree that it is difficult to find an actor not native to the area who can successfully master the precise nuances of the dialect. (Aa divvent knaa why not, like!)

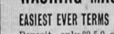

# CHAPTER 1

# The Origins of Geordie

To understand the origins of the Geordie dialect, it is necessary to *gan* back in time to the end of the 4th century AD. About this time, the Romans who had inhabited the area decided to leave. Consequently, the Celtic-speaking natives were left open to attack from the Picts. Feeling vulnerable, they decided to call for help and so found some *marras* from Denmark and Germany. The Anglo-Saxons, as we now call them, fought for their new friends in return for land, and brought with them a language which was quite distinctive. This language eventually formed the basis of the Geordie dialect and in fact, nowadays, most of the dialect words Geordies use are of Anglo-Saxon origin.

The meaning of *Geordie* has changed over the years. It once was said that only a person born in the immediate vicinity of Newcastle, just north of the river Tyne, could be called a *propa* Geordie. Indeed, even residents who live south of the Tyne may not always have been considered as true Geordies. However, in more recent years, the term has been applied more widely, to natives of Durham, Northumberland, and Tyne and Wear.

There are many theories as to why a Geordie is named as such. One of these theories is that they were named after the famous railway pioneer of the North, George Stevenson. Who knows for certain? One thing is sure, though, a good percentage of Geordies can be found assembled on the terraces of St James' Park on a Saturday afternoon cheering on their local *footbaal* team and shouting 'Toon Army'.

It is often said in Tyneside that *Wherever ye gan, ye will aalways meet a Geordie.* Back in 1992, my wife and I embarked upon on a trip to visit parents who were living in Australia at the time. While we were in the city of Perth, we took at trip for two days to Rottenest Island, a little island just off the south-west coast of Australia. There were very few people on the island at the time, and on our first evening we went to dine in the restaurant in the small hotel in which we were staying. After dinner, we ventured into the small bar in the hotel. There were only two other customers having a drink at the bar. As I ordered, one of them, hearing my accent, said:

'Are ye a Geordie?'

'Aye,' I replied.

'Whereaboots are ye from?' he asked.

'Newcastle,' I said.

'So am I!' said the man at the bar. 'Whereaboots in Newcastle?'

'Well, actually, more Gatesheed,' I replied.

'So am I!' said the man at the bar. 'I'm from Wardley.'

I was actually brought up in Wardley and so proceeded to tell him this.

'Well God!' he said. 'I cannit believe that! Which street did ye live in?'

'Thornley Avenue,' I said.

'Well I just moved from Cornforth Close last year,' he announced.

'Well would ye believe it?' I replied. 'That was where my wife lived for eleven years!'

'Blinkin hell!' he replied, 'what a small world!'

Looking back at that night, my wife and I wonder what odds we would have got from the bookmakers if we had by chance taken on a bet! We also wonder why we can never win the lottery!

# CHAPTER 2

# Traditional Tales and Folk Stuff

## THE BLAYDON RACES

There are many stories and songs that originate from the North-East of England, and, although they have been passed orally from generation to generation, they have also been written down for the future. One of the best-recorded Geordie traditions was the **Blaydon Races**. This was the name of the horse race meetings held on an island in the middle of the Tyne.

The last Blaydon race meeting was held on the 2nd September 1916. A riot broke out when a winning horse was disqualified, and the races were never held again.

On 5th June 1862, Geordie Ridley performed his song 'The Blaydon Races' for the first time at Balmbra's Music Hall in Newcastle. The song was sung at a

testimonial for Tyneside's sporting hero, British oarsman Harry Clasper. The words are as follows:

> I went to Blaydon races
> 'Twas on the ninth of June
> Eighteen hundred and sixty two
> On a summer's afternoon
> I took the bus from Balmbra's
> And she was heavy laden.
> Away we went along Collingwood Street
> To see the race at Blaydon.
>
> **Chorus:**
> Oh, me lads, you should've seen us gannin'
> Passing the folks along the road
> And all of them were starin'.
> All the lads and lasses there
> They all had smilin' faces
> Gannin' along the Scotswood Road
> To see the Blaydon races.
>
> We flew past Armstrong's factory
> And up by the Robin Adair
> But gannin' ower the Railway Bridge
> The bus wheel flew off there.
> The lasses lost their crinolenes
> And veils that hide their faces
> I got two black eyes and a broken nose
> In gannin' to Blaydon races.
>
> (Repeat Chorus)
>
> Now when we got the wheel back on
> Away we went again
> But them that had their noses broke
> They went back ower hyem.
> Some went to the dispensary
> And some to Doctor Gibbs
> And some to the infirmary
> To mend their broken ribs.

*(Repeat Chorus)*

We flew across the Chain Bridge
Reet into Blaydon Toon
The barman he was calling then
They called him Jackie Broon.
I saw him talking to some chaps
And them he was persuadin'
To gan and see Geordie Ridley's show
At the Mechanics' Hall in Blaydon.

Now when we got to Paradise
There were bonny games begun
There were four and twenty on the bus
And how we danced and sung.
They called on me to sing a song
So I sang 'em 'Paddy Fagan'
I danced a jig and I swung me twig
The day I went to Blaydon.

*(Repeat Chorus)*

The rain it poured down all the day
And made the ground quite muddy
Coffee Johnny had a white hat on
The old wife stole a cuddy.
There were spice stalls and monkey shows
And old wives selling ciders
And the chap on the ha'penny roundabout
Saying 'Any more lads for riders?'

*(Repeat Chorus)*

John Oliver or 'Coffee Johnny' as mentioned here in the last verse is generally considered to be a mythical person. However, he was actually a man who did exist, a man who was born, married and died in Winlaton. He was well known at the time as a bare knuckle fighter.

The original of The Blaydon Races painting by William Irving can be found at the Discovery Museum in Newcastle.

## WHEY AYE, MAN!

More recently, Irv Graham published a poem on the Toon Ale website, which can be sung to the tune of *The Blaydon Races* and refers to the changing landscape of the Tyne Valley:

Oh me lads ye shud'ave seen him gannin'
Gannin' alang the Scotchy Road with nee buildings stannin'
Nee mair lads or lasses there, nee boozers selling ale
Gannin' alang the Scotchy Road towards the Blaydon boot sale.
He took a walk from Balmbra's
His heart was heavey laden
Gannin' alang the Scotchy Road
That's on the way te Blaydon.
There's nee mair Cushy Butterfield,
Nee mair Robin Adair,
Nee mair Crooked Billet,
Nee boozers anywhere.
He got as far as Paradise yard
His legs were howldin' fine
Until I spied Vicors factory,
The new one by the Tyne.
He cudn't gan nee futher,
His heart was filled with woe.
What happened ti the people,
Where did aal the industry go?
He sat upon a grassy bank,
Bewildered he did stare;
Nee mair rows of hooses,
Nee community anywhere.
Nuw is this a thing caaled progress
Or a politicians lie?
A way of life disrupted
A way of life to die.
Oh me lads, ye shud ave seen him gannin'
Gannin' alang the Scotchy Road with nee buildings stannin'.
Nee mair lads or lasses there, nee boozers selling ale
Gannin' alang the Scotchy Road
Towards the Blaydon boot sale.

## Cushie Butterfield
by Geordie Ridley

I'm a broken hearted keelman, an' I'm o'er head in love,
With a young lass from Gateshead, an' I caal her me dove.
Her name is Cushie Butterfield, an' she sells yella clay,
An' her cousin is a muckman, an' they caal him Tom Gray.

**Chorus:**
She's a big lass, she's a bonny lass, an' she likes hor beer,
An' they caal her Cushie Butterfield, an' I wish she was here.

Her eyes are like two holes in a blanket pulled through,
An' her breath in the mornin' would scare a young coo.
An' when a hear 'er shoutin' – willya buy any clay?
Like a candyman's trumpet – steals me young heart away.

(*Chorus*)

Ye'll see her doon Sandgate when the fresh herring comes in,
She's like a bag full o' sawdust tied roond with a string.
She wears big galoshes, and 'er stockings was once white,
An' her bedgoon it's lilac, an' her hat's nivvor strite.

(*Chorus*)

When I asked her to marry uz, she started to laugh,
'Noo, nyen o' yer monkey tricks, for ah like nee sic chaff'.
Then she started a bubblin an' roared like a bull,
An' the chaps on the keel sez aa'm nowt but a fyeul.

(*Chorus*)

She said 'the chap that gets uz will have te work ivvery day,
An' when he comes hyem at neet, he'll have te gan an' seek clay.
An' when he's away seekin it, aall myek baalls an' sing,
O weel make the keel row that my laddie's in'.

(*Chorus*)

Both Cushie Butterfield and Tom Gray were real people. When Tom found out that Geordie Ridley had written this song for the local music hall, he was not amused. Rumour has it that he actually went gunning for Geordie!

## The Neighbours
### Written down by Edith May Douglas

They borra your onions, leeks and peas
Whenever they've got pots to boil.
They'll ask for ha'penny candles
When they canna get paraffin oil.
Whatever they borrow they never return.
Such folks I never saw.
They'd skin a rat for it's hide and fat,
The neighbours down belaw.

## Keep Yer Feet Still, Geordie Hinny
### (traditional song)

Wor Geordie and Bob Johnson byeth lay i' one bed
In a little loggin' hoose done the shore.
Before he'd been an hour asleep a kick from Geordie's fut
Made him waken up to roar i'stead o'snore.

**Chorus**:
Keep yor feet still Geordie Hinny,
Let's be happy for the neet,
For aa may not be so happy thro the day.
So give us that bit comfort,
Keep yor feet still Geordie lad
And divvent drive me bonny dreams away.

Aa dreamt thor wes a dansin' held an' Mary Clark was there
An' aa thowt we tript leetly on the floor,
An' aa prest hor heevin breest te mine when waisin' roon the room
Tha's mair than aa dor ivver de afore.

### The Ji-Jaller Bag

This folk tale has been passed down over the years.

In a village not so far from Newcastle, a long long time ago, there lived an old hag. She was a thief and had robbed the villagers for years. No one could prove that she was responsible for the thefts, but they were fairly sure. She lived by herself in a little cottage, but, as she grew older, she found that she could no longer keep her house clean by herself, so she hired a servant girl. She told the girl to rise early and sweep out her house but not the chimney. Each night she would tell the girl, 'If you poke about in the chimney, all the soot will fall and we'll have a fine mess to be sure!'

Usually the girl did just as she was instructed, leaving the chimney alone and cleaning everywhere else. However, one day, before the old woman was awake, the girl put her brush up the chimney and down fell a bag of money. The girl did not stop to look inside, but quickly turned toward the door and ran outside, leaving the old woman still sleeping. Very soon, the girl came to a gate. To her surprise the gate spoke and said to her:

> 'Pretty maid, oh pretty maid
> Open me I pray,
> For I've not been open
> For many a long day!'

But the girl tossed her head and said, 'Open yourself gate, I have no time.'

Then she turned and kept on going. Soon she met a cow standing to one side of the path, and the cow too spoke to the girl:

> 'Pretty maid, oh pretty maid
> Milk me I pray,
> For I've not been milked
> For many a long day!'

But the girl tossed her head and said, 'Milk yourself cow, I have no time.'

Then she turned and kept on going. Soon she came to a mill at one side of the path, and the mill too spoke to the girl:

> 'Pretty maid, oh pretty maid
> Turn me I pray,
> For I've not been turned
> For many a long day!'

But the girl tossed her head and said, 'Turn yourself mill, I have no time.'

By this time she was so tired she hid the bag in the mill-hopper and went to sleep.

Meanwhile the old woman had woken up to find her money gone.

'My ji-jaller bag! My wee leather bag!' she cried. Then she grabbed her shawl from the chair and hurried after the girl. Soon she came to the gate.

> 'Gate o' mine, gate so fine,
> Have you seen that girl o' mine
> Wi' a ji-jaller bag
> And a wee leather bag
> Wi' all the money in it
> That I ever had?'

And the gate said, 'Farther on ...' The old woman walked along until she met the cow.

> 'Cow o' mine, cow so fine,
> Have you seen that girl o' mine
> Wi' a ji-jaller bag
> And a wee leather bag
> Wi' all the money in it
> That I ever had?'

And the cow said, 'Farther on . . .' The old woman walked along until she met the mill.

> 'Mill o' mine, mill so fine,
> Have you seen that girl o' mine
> Wi' a ji-jaller bag
> And a wee leather bag
> Wi' all the money in it
> That I ever had?'

And the mill said, 'In the hopper!' So the old woman walked around the back of the mill, opened the hopper, and found the girl and all the money again.

The very next day she hired a new girl to do the housework, and once again told her not to clean the chimney. Well, the new girl had already heard that the last housemaid found the stolen money up the chimney; so as soon as the old woman fell asleep she took the bag down and ran off with it. She wanted to give the money back to its rightful owners. This time, when the girl came to the gate, she opened it. When she came to the cow, she milked it, and, when she came to the mill, she turned it. Then she ran off down the hill to the village. When the old woman woke up she set off after the girl, but, when she asked the gate if it had seen the girl, the gate said nothing. When she asked the cow if it had seen the girl, the cow said nothing. And when she asked the mill if it had seen the girl, the mill said nothing. So the girl escaped with the money and the people of the village shared it out.

# CHAPTER 3

## Scran and Ale

'Pease Pudding hot, pease pudding cold.
Pease pudding in the pot nine days old.
Some like it hot, some like it cold.
Some like it in the pot nine days old.'

*Traditional North Country rhyme.*

There are many traditional foods that originate from Tyneside. Some foods are now not as popular as they used to be and others are still going strong in the region. If you visit any supermarket or food store these days, you will almost certainly be able to find one of our more popular local delicacies: **pease pudding.** At some time or another, many a grandmother across the North-East will have made this thick yellow substance and will have served it hot or cold.

### Ingredients

1 large potato
8 oz yellow split peas
4 oz bacon or ham scraps
    without rind
1 skinned onion
1 egg, beaten
1 teaspoon sugar
black pepper
salt
chopped parsley (a posh option!)

## Method

Wash and drain the peas. Tie them loosely along with the potato in a piece of cloth or muslin. Put in a pan and cover with fresh cold water. Add the ham or bacon scraps and the onion. Bring to the boil, skim and boil gently for two hours or until tender. Drain the peas and potatoes and pick out the onion as much as possible. Mix the mixture with the butter, egg, sugar and a little pepper and salt. When this is smooth, add the parsley (if you want the more upper-class version) and turn this into a mould or a warm serving dish.

Finally, if ye are feeling a bit peckish, then scoff the lot!

Another north-eastern recipe which is still *gannin'* strong is the *stottie cyek*. Eat a full one of these and you feel like you don't need to eat again for a week! **Stottie cakes** can best be described as large, flat bread buns. They are often used for sandwiches and can be spotted on many a mobile food van at car-boot sales on a Sunday morning. There is a particular art to making a perfect stottie ... *gan on*, give it a try!

### Ingredients

2lbs strong plain flour

3 level tsp. salt

3 oz margarine

1$\frac{1}{2}$ oz fresh yeast or 3 level tsp. dried yeast

1 tsp. sugar

$\frac{1}{2}$ pint tepid water – (not too hot)

$\frac{1}{2}$ pint milk

This makes 3$\frac{1}{4}$ lbs of dough. The precise quantity of liquid required varies, but the dough should be firm but pliable and not too stiff.

## Method

Mix the flour and salt together and rub in the margarine. Mix the yeast and sugar into the water, stirring until the yeast dissolves. If you use dry yeast, mix the yeast and sugar into the water and leave until the yeast has dissolved and is frothy. Make a little hole in the centre of the flour and add the water, working the mixture into a firm dough with your hands. Knead well until the dough is smooth and shiny. Turn it out onto a floured board

and knead until it is no longer sticky and is smooth and shiny. Lightly grease a dish and place dough in it; cover with a tea-towel and leave to rise in a warm place until it is twice the size, or you could put it in a large plastic bag. Heat the oven to 425°F/220°C. When risen turn onto floured board and knead lightly to let out the air and to make the dough pliable again. Cut the dough to the size of the stottie you want. Put a hole in the middle of the stottie after rolling it out to the size and depth required and with a fork make a few stabs (not too many). Place the stotties on a baking sheet and bake near the top of the oven for 12 to 15 minutes. It may take a little longer but don't leave in too long. Test with a fork: if it comes out clean, they're done! If the fork is sticky, then they need to be cooked for a bit *langer*; so stick them back in the oven!

The **singin' hinnie**, another dish which originated from the north-east, is so called because when the butter and cream melt during baking, a sizzling can be heard. Many have said that the sound is like singing. An old tale is told of how this large tea-time scone first became known as a singing hinnie;

*A bairn asks his mutha who is cooking griddle scones 'Why is it making that strange noise?' His mutha replies: 'It's singing, hinny!' (Hinny is a Geordie term of endearment.)*

### Ingredients

8 oz plain flour
4 oz butter
1 tsp baking powder
7 fl oz milk
pinch of salt
handful of currants

### Method

Mix the flour, butter, salt, and baking powder in a food processor for about 1 minute. The aim is not a thorough blend, but to leave small granules of butter in the mixture.

Transfer to a mixing bowl and add the milk and currants to form a stiff dough. Roll out into about six thin, flat scones. Separate with greaseproof paper and freeze.

Cook from frozen on a very hot griddle, with the thinnest layer of butter possible. (Try to remove as much as you can using a kitchen towel.) Turn occasionally until cooked through. Eat immediately with butter and raspberry jam.

Finally, there is another dish, by the name of **Pan Haggerty**, which is a speciality of the North-East. This is a wholesome dish, which is best served straight from the pan.

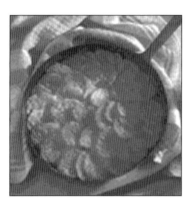

### Ingredients
1lb (450g) potatoes
4oz (110g) Cheddar or Lancashire cheese
2 medium onions
1 oz (26g) butter
1 tbsp vegetable oil
salt and pepper

## Method
Thinly slice the potatoes and onions and grate the cheese. Combine the butter and oil in a large frying pan. Remove the pan from the heat and place layers of potatoes, onions and cheese, reserving a little of the cheese. Cover and cook gently for about 30mins or until the potatoes and onions are cooked. Pre-heat the grill 5mins before the end of the cooking time. Sprinkle the reserved cheese over the top of the mixture. Place under grill until the cheese is golden brown and bubbling.

Pan Haggerty is best eaten on a winter's eve when the weather outside is less than desirable. If eaten straight from the pan, you will have a lovely warm feeling inside.

Well now that you have your traditional Geordie food, why not have the perfect accompaniment? . . .

## ALE
Tynesiders don't have a great number of home grown beverages, but one thing is for sure: Ye cannit come to Newcastle without trying the locally brewed Newcastle Brown Ale!

Also known as 'Newkie broon' and just plain 'broon', this ale has been produced on Tyneside since 1927. The brew was produced in Newcastle's Tyne

Brewery until recently, when it moved across the river and is now made in the Federation Brewery in Dunston, Gateshead. This is not an ale in the traditional sense of the word but has certainly helped to put Newcastle on the map over the years. The brew has PGI (protected Geographical Indication) from the European Union, which ensures that this beverage may be produced only on Tyneside. However, the company are applying to have this protection lifted and this would then allow them to brew the ale outside the area. In the UK, Newcastle Brown Ale is the biggest selling premium bottled ale. It is also one of the fastest growing imported beers in the United States, where sales are climbing by an average of 12% each year, and it is exported to 40 countries worldwide.

Furthermore, the distinctive taste has recently become the latest ice cream flavour. Produced by Doddington Dairies, a family run dairy farm, the ice cream will be available only during the summer months. The makers say that the handmade ice cream reflects the region's identity. It was handed out to the European Capital of Culture judges on

their last visit. The preparation process means that the ice cream contains less than 1% alcohol.

Many a club and pub sell this strongly flavoured alcoholic beverage, and many Tynesiders feel a sense of home pride when they drink it! Like it or loathe it, when ye come te Newcastle, ye've gorra try it!

# "GAN AN GIT YERSEL ON THE TOON YE DIVVENT KNA WHAT YER MISSIN"

Another home grown ale is the 'Toon Ale'. First brewed in 1922 and made in two varieties. Toon Ale Blonde and Toon Ale Brunette. Both have their own distinctive flavours.

*Light and quenching with a somewhat bitter edge. A 'hoppy' flourish with a twist of lime undertone*

*A complex natural rich old Brown Ale. Subtle 'hoppiness' with a velvety smooth taste and a subtle caramel note.*

### HOW CAN YOU RESIST?

# CHAPTER 4

## A Reet Canny Laff

**W**ell, what can I say about Geordie comedians? Over the years Tyneside has been blessed with many. I enjoy laughing at a lot of different comedians and find jokes and little ditties very amusing. However, particular favourites of mine are Bobby Thompson, The Dixielanders, and Alan Snell. The reason I am attracted to their humour is simple: they are blessed with the ability to laugh at their own situations and to turn bleak issues into side splitting tales.

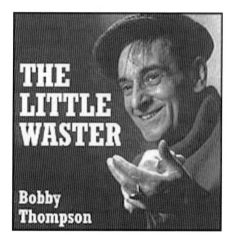

THE LITTLE WASTER

Bobby Thompson

**Bobby Thompson** was born in 1910 and appeared in working men's clubs for some 20 years.

Bobby was a man who attributed his wife, or *Wor Lass*, the unique talent of being able to 'yodel with a dinna plate in hor mooth'. He also told the story of a letter he received from the bank stating he was £642 overdrawn. Bobby said: 'Aa didn't write te them when they had *my* money!'

The **Dixielanders** were a comedy duo, Billy Martin and Bobby Hopper, who performed around the North-East. In the late 1970s, they launched the

Dixielanders' Music Hall, and James Bolam and Malcolm McDonald were among the celebrities at the opening night.

Much of the pair's humour was around poverty. They would tell of nights in the 'olden days' when they stood inside the fish and chip shop 'cos it was warmer than in the hoose'. Billy would also tell of how he 'escaped from Gateshead' by swimming across the Tyne.

In 1979, a recording of the show, entitled 'The Fabulous Dixielanders' was issued as an album. This was recently re-released on CD and cassette and has proved to be in demand still. Unfortunately, Billy died in 2002.

**Q.** Who was born in a stable and followed by millions?

**A.** *Red Rum.*

This is just one of the many one-liners from **Alan Snell**, another great north-eastern comic. He hails from Gateshead and was a member of a vocal group, The Langford Boys, before switching to comedy in 1970. His ill-fitting outfit of black suit and white vest makes him instantly recognizable.

Again, like other north-eastern comics, Alan talks of poverty in the 'olden days' and recalls how his family was so poor they were well practised in making money in any way they could. He claimed that they could even 'sell pegs to the gypsies'.

# CHAPTER 5

## Stories from Geordieland

**M**uch of Geordie humour relates to the working men's clubs of the region, and often if jokes are not set in the club then they make some reference to drinking. These are topics which make us Gerodies laugh and, for this reason, I have decided to include a sampling of such jokes in this section. Enjoy!

### GANNIN ON A CRUISE, LIKE

Geordie and his marra had a big win on the lottery. So they decided to gan on a world cruise. After a week at sea, the captain called the purser into his cabin to ask what respected people were on board, so that he could invite them to his table. 'Sir,' said the purser, 'we have four pop stars, three doctors, and two strange gentlemen from the North who seem to be very wealthy.' The captain told him to go round with invitations.

Hoy, is that a bottle of Broon?

Knocking on the Geordies' cabin door, he was greeted by 'Hello, Bonny Lad, howay in.' When he entered, there was Geordie and his marra – feet and four broon ale on the table – eating fish and chips. The purser saluted, 'Begging your pardon, gentlemen,' he said, 'the captain requests your company at his table tonight.'

'Ye must be joking,' says Geordie. 'Ye divvent think wi gan te spend aal this money to eat with the bloody crew!'

## GEORDIE GANS TE THE CLUB

Geordie went to the CIU club, 'coz he is "filleted", ye knaa'; he hord there was gan a be a magic torn on like.

Well, anyway, the magician came on and was pulling eggs oot of ears, pigeons oot of hankies – the lot. Whey Geordie was well impressed, so much so that at the end of the act he went up to the magician and said: 'By hinny! Aa didn't knaa ye woz so good like.'

The magician said: 'Did ye like my act, Geordie?'

'Whey aye aa did! Ye'd gan a bomb at the Legion on a Sunday morning, 30 bob and ya beer like.'

'Then,' said the magician, 'would you be surprised if I put my hand in your jacket pocket and pulled a rabbit out?'

'I waald, an aal,' says Geordie. 'I've got a ferret in there.'

## GEORDIE FANCIES SOME NEW SHOES, LIKE

One night Geordie was having a pint in the club, when he seen a bloke with a very unusual pair of shoes on. Geordie couldn't keep his eyes off them. So he says to the bloke, 'Hoy mista! What kind a shoes is them ye have on? Aad like to hev a pair of them, like'.

'They're crocodile shoes,' said the gent.

'Whey aa nivvor,' says Geordie. 'Aam sorry if a soond a bit thick, like, but what's a crocodile?'

'Well,' says the gent, 'a crocodile is a reptile, which inhabits the rivers of Africa; the River Zambezi is full of them.'

'Thanks, mista!' says Geordie. 'Aa'll have te hev a pair of them.'

So Geordie gives the club a miss for a wee while to save enough money to book a flight to Africa. Paddling his dingy up the river, he sees a huge crocodile. Geordie being a big bloke, strips off doon to his kecs, and swims knife between his teeth to the croc. He fights it, kills it, drags it ashore, looks at it, and says, 'Ah, bugger! Aal that trouble and it's got nee shoes on.'

## GEORDIE IN AN AMERICAN PIT

Well aal the pits seemed to be closing up North and Geordie was made redundant. Reading the papers the next day, he sees an advert: *Miners wanted in U.S.A., two hundred dollars per week, house and car supplied.* So off he gans to the U.S.A. First day at the pit, going down the cage, the cage stops. Geordie

says to an American, 'Hoy, Lad, is this where wi start diggin? Is this the coal fyce?'

'You must be that new guy from England,' says the Yank.

'Aye, am from Gatesheed, son,' says Geordie.

'Well, Bud, you don't start here: you wait here, and an old diesel train comes along; you jump on and stay on and endure a two and a half hour ride.'

After the ride Geordie says to the Yank, 'De ye mek a start noo, Hinny?'

'No, Bud,' says the Yank. 'You stand here, another train comes, you have another two hour ride'.

This goes on all day, 8 o'clock in the morning till 5 o'clock at night. Geordie nivvor lifted a pick. He couldn't stand it nee more, 'Hoy, Bonny Lad,' he says to the Yank, 'I've had enough of this, it's warse than working, I'm gannin back hyem the morra.'

'You can't leave us now,' says the Yank. 'We are at war with Vietnam!'

'They've bloody good reet,' says Geordie. 'Yiv dug that far oot ye pinchin' tha coal!'

## THE WRANG NAME TO HEV

I remember gannin' to the Bigg Market for a few beers with me marras. Well, as normally happens at 'chuckin oot time', a scrap starts and beer bottles start to fly. Well aa noticed the lad in front of me was dookin' and dodgin', so aa says to him, 'It's ne good ye dein that, Lad. If one of them bottles has your name on, ye'll get it.'

'Aye aa knaa – that's wot am worried aboot,' he says. 'Me name's McEwan!'

## NOT DEED CLIVVOR LIKE

One day, when Geordie was doon toon, he sees a geet big funeral coming up the Haymarket: brass band; four plumed horses pulling the hearse; three coaches, and aboot 1,000 mourners waalking behind it. 'Whey, he must be an

important bloke,' he thinks to himsel. 'A lord mayor or chief of police or summik. Aa knaa, he thinks, a'll ask this paper lad: he'll knaa who it is.

'Hoy, young un!' says Geordie. 'D'ye knaa who it is that's deed ower yonder?'

'Whey,' says the paper lad. 'If aa had te put a bet on it like, aad say the bloke in the coffin.'

## THE WRANG BIKE

Young Geordie's oot on the toon with his marras. They aal decide to gan to the neet club and see if they can tap up some skirt. Well, Geordie meets a lass and as the neet gans on he thinks he's on a promise. At chuckin' oot time Geordie thinks it's time to mek his move.

'D'ye fancy comin' back to mine, like?' he says.

'A cannit, Geordie, aam on me menstrual cycle,' says the lass.

'Divvent worry, pet,' says Geordie, 'aave got me motor bike – aal just follow ye!'

## ME MUTHA MAKES A SPECTACLE OF ASEL

I remember when a was a youngun and me and wor family went on a camping holiday te Devon. There was me Mutha, Fatha, Brutha, me Uncle and Aunt, three Cousins, Grandmutha and Grandfatha, so quite a few of wi.

Well just to put ye in the picture, on wor forst day wi aal decided to gan to the local toon for some bait and stuff, well me uncle had one of those sharts on with the chest pocket and he aalways stuck his reedin glasses in them when he waasn't using them. Well anyway, wi aal needed to cross ower the road, but being a lot of wi, annly half of wi managed to cross ower before a car came.

Me uncle was one of them left on the other side of the road, but me mutha had managed to cross. Well, when she was waiting on the other side she looked ower to me uncle and noticed his glasses were hanging oot of his shart pocket, ready to faal. This was on a very busy Satday and me mutha bein the sort who aalways gets a wards mixed up. Decided to try and waarn me uncle that his glasses were aboot to faal oot of his pocket. Whey a divvent knaa whether me mutha was trying te sooned clever or what by tryin to use the ward spectacles instead of glasses, but she managed ti mix it up with the ward tenticles and thereby shooted reet across the crooded street at the top of a voice.

'Hoy Michael ye testicles are hanging oot.' Whey ye knaa, me poor aad uncle went bright reed.

Bus Stop Scene 3

*Whey ye bugger!*

RS

# CHAPTER 6

# Places Te Gan in Geordieland

## CROSSIN' THE WATTA

The North-East is a region full of attractions. The city of Newcastle itself stands on the banks of the River Tyne, which is crossed by a number of bridges. The **Millennium Bridge** is the newest addition. Opened on 17th September 2001, the bridge was the first tilting bridge to be built across the Tyne in more than 100 years. With its unique 'blinking eye' mechanism, the bridge has attracted worldwide attention. The £22 million structure carries a footpath and a cycle track to link the Gateshead and Newcastle quays.

Although the Millennium Bridge is very impressive, the most famous of the bridges is the **Tyne Bridge**, standing majestically over the river. When it opened, in 1928, the Tyne Bridge was the largest single-span bridge in the world. This magnificent title was retained for four years until the Sydney Harbour Bridge was

*Gateshead Millennium Bridge.*

opened in 1932. The two bridges are very similar in design, and many claim that the Sydney Harbour Bridge is a copy of the Tyne Bridge. However, the truth is that the designs for the Tyne Bridge were submitted later than those for the Sydney Harbour Bridge.

## *Cummin hyem* by Irv Graham

> Grand it is to see yon
> Each and every line,
> Oh canny bridge that spans
> Rippled wattors of the Tyne,
> Doon aal the roads aah've trod
> In ivorry city aah did stem
> Echoed voices of Newcastle
> Singing hinny let's gan hyem
> Back across the Tyne Bridge
> Among Geordie folk once mair.
> Come on wandering laddie
> Knaa ye yer heart lies there.

The total number of bridges that span the River Tyne is now seven. A visitor to the region could therefore be sure he would have no difficulty in finding his way across the watta!

*Tyne Bridge, Newcastle-Upon-Tyne.*

One thing, though, that goes without saying, is that the landscape of the Tyne valley has changed a great deal over the years. Irv Graham wrote a poem about this.

## Tyne Valley

Aah stood upon a grassy bank,
Looked across the valley of the Tyne,
And me heart was filled with pleasure
To see the heritage that is mine.
Men of iron, hearts of oak,
Salt water in their veins –
A folk who are rough diamonds
And never show their pains.
They took away the coal mines;
They took away the steel;
They took away the fishing;
And the community it did reel.
But we pulled ourselves together
And made it a party toon;
Now the whole world's singing
'Oh for a bottle of Toon'.
The Bigg Market and the Quayside,
We welcome you all there,
Come taste a Geordie evening,
A Geordie night to share.
If you stood upon a grassy bank
To view the valley of the Tyne
I know that you'd be wishing
To share with me what's mine.

## OOT AND ABOOT ON THE BOOZE

If you come to Tyneside for nightlife, then you cant go far wrong! In fact, people from all over the country come to sample the pubs and clubs of Newcastle. The choice of hostelries is excellent. There are many fantastic places to wine and dine. One of them is the **Bigg Market**. Although quieter from Monday to Thursday, this is where the younger of us party regularly on weekend evenings. Even with approximately 20 bars in this area alone, there is often a queue forming outside most pubs on the more popular evenings. At the bottom end of the Bigg

*'Gis a pint please, marra!'*

A typical Bigg Market drink

*'A cheeky cocktail'*

A Quayside preference

Market is Balmbra's, which stands on the site of the old music hall. It was here that the first performance of the famous song 'The Blaydon Races' took place in 1862. Although the majority of hostelries in this area are drinking bars only, there are numerous restaurants and take-aways nearby. Without much effort, you can have one too many pints and then roll down the road or round the corner and grab a tasty kebab, an al-funghi pizza or a korma to drop on your new white shirt – highly attractive, but the trademark of an extremely rebellious night out!

*Hoy, geet the roond in man!*

The Cooperage, Newcastle-Upon-Tyne.

The **Quayside** is another popular area of Newcastle in which to wine and dine. It is fast becoming the place to be seen in Newcastle, and, although young and old are welcome, it is generally patronized by the more mature. The choice of pubs is excellent, ranging from the new up-market Pitcher and Piano at one end to the 14th-century Cooperage at the other. There is also a fine selection of restaurants, making it an ideal place to dine out.

## FINDING CULTCHA

Well one thing is for sure, the Geordies 'like a bit of cultcha, ye knaa!' The impressive **Angel of the North** is Britain's largest sculpture. Standing near the A1

*The Angel of the North, Gateshead.*

in Gateshead, it towers 20 metres above the landscape and has a wingspan of 54 metres.

The Angel was created by Anthony Gormley, an internationally renowned sculptor, and was assembled on site in February 1998. It is made of 200 tonnes of steel. In May 1998, the famous Angel was bedecked by the famous No 9 shirt of Alan Shearer, but not for long!

**Gateshead Quays** houses a number of cultural venues, and in December 2004 the **Sage Music Centre** took its place as the region's new home for music and musical discovery. A £70 million project, the centre is home to the Northern Sinfonia orchestra, and also provides unique facilities for people of all ages to learn, listen to, and make

music. The 1,650-seat concert hall is designed with superior acoustics (so that even a Geordie with a few pints in his system can sound like Frank Sinatra), and the building's glass frontage offers fantastic views across the River Tyne.

Within a stone's throw of the Sage,

*The Sage, Gateshead.*

*Baltic, Gateshead.*

stands the **Baltic** centre for contemporary arts. Originally a flourmill, Baltic was opened as a 'public art space' in July 2002. With a rooftop restaurant that offers splendid views of Tyneside, the building accommodates 3,000 sq m of art space and houses five galleries, a cinema/lecture space, artists' studios, a media lab and a library for study.

## SHOP TILL YA DROP

There are many facilities for the discerning shopper on Tyneside, and right in the heart of Newcastle is **Northumberland Street**, its main street. It was once part of the main London to Edinburgh route until the building of the city bypass. Over the centuries, the street has been served by horse-drawn stagecoaches, trams, trolley buses, and petrol buses, but, is now dominated by a pedestrianized walkway. In 1932 the high street giant Marks & Spencer graced the street with its presence, and gradually over the years, Northumberland Street has grown to accommodate most high-street stores. One of its main attractions is the Fenwick store, a department store which now famously has an animated and musical window display at Christmas time.

*Northumberland Street, Newcastle-Upon-Tyne.*

## FOOTBAAL

*St James's Park, Newcastle-Upon-Tyne.*

Well, it goes without saying, Geordies 'luv footbaal' and are very passionate supporters of their home team, Newcastle United. Week after week supporters grace the terraces of St James's Park.

Nicknamed 'the Magpies', Newcastle United supporters are also known as the 'Toon Army', a term they frequently chant when watching their team play. Over the years, the team has had a number of exceptional players. Amongst others, there has been, Jackie Milburn, Malcolm MacDonald, Kevin Keegan, Paul Gascoigne, Alan Shearer, Michael Owen, Obafemi Martins and Mark Viduka .

Equally, the team has also sported some notable managers, including:

| | |
|---|---|
| Joe Kinnear | (2008–2009) |
| Sam Allardyce | (2007–2008) |
| Glenn Roeder | (2006–2007) |
| Graeme Souness | (2004–2006) |
| Sir Bobby Robson | (1999–2004) |
| Ruud Gullit | (1998–1999) |
| Kenny Dalglish | (1997–1998) |
| Kevin Keegan | (1992–1997) |
| Osvaldo Ardiles | (1991–1992) |
| Jim Smith | (1988–1991) |

| | |
|---|---|
| Willie McFaul | (1985–1988) |
| Jack Charlton | (1984) |
| Arthur Cox | (1980–1984) |
| Bill McGarry | (1977–1980) |
| Richard Dinnis | (1977) |
| Gordon Lee | (1975–1977) |
| Joe Harvey | (1962–1975) |
| Norman Smith | (1961–1962) |
| Charlie Mitten | (1958–1961) |
| Stan Seymour | (1956–1958) |
| Duggie Livingstone | (1954–1956) |
| Stan Seymour | (1950–1954) |
| George Martin | (1947–1950) |
| Stan Seymour | (1939–1947) |
| Tom Mather | (1935–1939) |
| Andy Cunningham | (1930–1935) |
| Frank Watt | (1895–1932) |

The club was officially named as Newcastle United Football Club Co Ltd on 6th September 1895. The present terraces were built as part of a regeneration programme, and the ground now comprises the East Stand, the Leazes Stand, the Newcastle Brown or Gallowgate End, and the Milburn Stand.

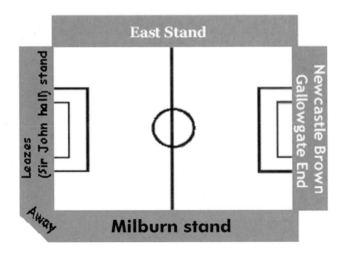

# A Local Neb at Nursery Rhymes

## Little Miss Muffet

# CHAPTER 7

## Dicshinery

**aa** = I
*Aa divvent knaa.* 'I don't know.'
**aad** = old
**aaful** = awful
**aal** = all
**aald** = old
*aald fella* 'old man'
**aam** = I am
**aarn** = own
**agyen** = again
**ahaad** (to) hold
**alang** = along
**amang** = among
**aye** yes
**ayont** behind
**baad** = bad, i.e. ill
**baal** = ball
**bagie** a turnip
**bairn** baby, child
**bait** food
**barra** barrow
**behint** = behind
**blaa** = blow
**bleb** a spot
**bonny** pretty, beautiful

Hoy, Mista! Canna hev me **baal** back?

| | |
|---|---|
| **bord** | = bird |
| **borst** | = burst |
| | *He's borst the baal.* 'He's burst the ball.' |
| **brass** | money |
| **breed** | = bread |
| **breeks** | trousers |
| **breyk** | = break |
| **broon** | = brown |
| **bumbla** | bee |
| **caad** | = cold |
| | *It's caad oot there.* 'It's cold out there.' |
| **caal** | = coal |
| **canna** | = can't, cannot |
| **canny** | nice |
| | *She's deed canny.* 'She's very nice' |
| **cyek** | = cake |
| **chaak** | = chalk |
| **champion** | good; brilliant |
| **chare** | lane |
| **charver** | (young) scoundrel, rogue |
| **chimley** | chimney |
| **chorch** | = church |
| **claa** | = claw |
| **claes** | = clothes |
| | *Aa've got nae claes.* 'I've got no clothes.' |
| **clag** | to stick |
| **clarty** | muddy; sticky |
| **clivvor** | = clever |
| **coo** | = cow |
| **craa** | = crow |
| **crood** | = crowd |
| **croon** | = crown |

| | |
|---|---|
| **cuddy** | horse |
| **cyuk** | = cook |
| **dafty** | a silly person (used affectionately) |
| | *Yer a reet dafty.* 'You are a very silly person' |
| **deed** | = dead |
| **deef** | = deaf |
| **disn't** | = doesn't |
| **divvent** | = don't |
| **doon** | = down |
| **dorty** | = dirty |
| **dowie** | depressed |
| **dowta** | = daughter |
| **droond** | = drowned |
| **dunch** | to bump (into), collide with (used especially when driving) |
| | *Divvent dunch uz.* 'Don't bump into me.' |
| **faal** | fall |
| **femmer** | weak |
| **fettle** | condition; mood |
| | *in a fettle* in a mood |
| **fower** | = four |
| **fret** | a sea mist |
| **fyul** | = fool |
| **gan** | (to) go |
| **gannin'** | going |
| | *Aam gannin' te the shops.* 'I am going to the shops.' |
| **gandie** | a look |
| **ganzie** | jumper |
| **gaumless** | stupid, silly |
| **gawk** | to stare |
| | *Wot are ye gawkin' at?* 'What are you staring at?' |

What ye **gawkin** at?

| | |
|---|---|
| **geet** | very |
| **git** | = get |
| **giveower!** | = give over! |
| | *Giveower, Man* 'I don't believe you!' |
| **giz** | = give |
| **gor** | = got |
| **gowk** | applecore |
| **granda** | grandfather |
| **gyet** | = gate |
| **haad** | (to) hold |
| | *Git haad of it.* 'Get hold of it.' |
| **haadin'** | = holding |
| **hack** | cough |
| **hacky** | dirty |
| | *He's hacky dorty.* 'He's really dirty.' |
| **hadaway!** | go away!, begone!; get away (with you)! |
| **howay!** | 'come on!' |
| | *Haway, Man!* 'Come with me!' |
| **heed** | = head |
| **heor** | = here, hear |
| **hinny** | a term of affection |
| | *me hinny* 'my darling' |
| **hippin** | nappy |
| **hoppings** | a fair; specifically a traditional travelling fair that visits Newcastle's Town Moor every summer |
| **howdy** | midwife |
| **howk** | to pull |
| | *Howk it out.* 'Pull it out' |
| **hoy** | to throw, fling |
| **hyem** | = home |
| **impittent** | = impudent; cheeky |
| **insteed** | = instead |
| **ivvor** | = ever |

| | |
|---|---|
| **jaa** | = jaw |
| **kite** | belly, stomach |
| **knaa** | = (to) know |
| **knaarn** | = known |
| | *I've knaarn him for ages.* 'I've known him for a long time.' |
| **knackin'** | hurting |
| **knive** | gully |
| **laa** | = low |
| | *Laa-level bridge* 'Low-level bridge' |
| **lad** | boy, man |
| **lang** | long |
| **larn** | = learn |
| **lass** | girl, woman |
| | *wor lass* 'my girlfriend/wife' |
| **liggy** | a marble |
| **lop** | flea |
| **lowp** | =leap |
| **lug** | ear |
| | *Me lug is knackin uz.* 'My ear is hurting.' |
| **mair** | = more |
| **marra** | friend, mate |
| | *He's me marra.* 'He's my friend'. |
| **mebbies** | = maybe |
| **mint** | fantastic |
| **misdoot** | doubt |
| **nae** | no |
| **naebody** | nobody |
| **neet** | night |
| **netty** | a toilet |
| **nivvor** | = never |
| **nowt** | nothing |
| | *Aa've got nowt.* 'I've got nothing' |

| | |
|---|---|
| **nyem** | = name |
| **oot** | = out |
| **ootside** | = outside |
| | *Let's gan ootside.* 'Let's go outside' |
| **ower** | = over |
| **owld** | = old |
| **pallatic** | paralytic, i.e. extremely intoxicated |
| **penker** | a marble |
| **pittle** | to urinate |
| **ploat** | to pluck |
| **plodge** | to wade |
| **prog** | to prick |
| **put** | to throb, palpitate |
| **raa** | = row |
| **rang** | = wrong |
| **reed** | = red |
| **reet** | = right |
| **sackless** | useless |
| | *He's deed sackless.* 'He's quite useless' |
| **scabby** | shabby |
| **scad** | scald |
| **scoor** | = scour |
| **scran** | food |
| **shan** | unfair |
| **shart** | = shirt |
| **short** | = shirt |
| **slip** | pinafore |
| **snaa** | = snow |
| **sneck** | latch, catch |
| **spuggy** | a sparrow |
| **stot** | to bounce |
| | *Stot the baal off the waal.* 'Bounce the ball off the wall.' |

| | |
|---|---|
| **straa** | = straw |
| **tab** | cigarette |
| | *Do ye want a tab?* 'Do you want a cigarette?' |
| **tackle** | to accost; to ask specifically about an issue. |
| | *Aa tackled him aboot it.* 'I asked him about it.' |
| **tappy-lappy** | carefree |
| **tatty** | tangled |
| | *Me hair is aal tatty.* 'My hair is all tangled' |
| **te** | = to |
| **tetty** | potato |
| **Toon** | Newcastle United Football Club |
| **tyek** | = take |
| **uz** | me; us |
| | *Are ye comin' with uz?* 'Are you coming with me/us?' |
| **waard** | = word |
| **waark** | = work |
| **watta** | = water |
| **whey aye** | definitely, most certainly, yes |
| | *Whey aye, Man!* |
| **wisht** | quiet |
| **withoot** | without |
| | *Aa divvent knaa wot aa'd de withoot ye.* 'I don't know what I'd do without you' |
| **wor** | = our |
| **wors** | = ours |
| **yammer** | to chatter, gossip; to whine, complain |
| **ye** | you |
| **yeeam** | = home |
| **yersel** | = yourself |

The **wattas** a bit caad like!

# CHAPTER 8

## A Gandie at Geordie Phrases

**Can ye tyek me gowk oot?**
Please can you remove the core from my apple?

**The bairn has borst his baal.**
The child has burst his ball.

**That impittent kid is in a right fettle.**
That cheeky child is a little moody today!

**Whey aye, ye can hinny!**
Of course you can, my darling!

**Me left lug is really knacking uz!**
My left ear is extremely sore!

**Me gaffer is mint!**
My foreman is an extremely fine fellow!

**Where are ye gannin' the neet?**
Where are you going to this fine evening?

**Aam gannin' yeeam cos am a bit boozed up!**
I am going home because I am a little under the influence.

**Aa knaa, me marra.**
I know, my friend.

**Those gobstoppas breyk ya jaa, ye knaa!**
Those very large sweeties hurt your jaw. Don't eat them.

**Those gullies are very sharp, ye knaa!**
I think you had better be careful because those knives can be very dangerous!

**Aave gor a gammy leg, ye knaa, so a cannit lowp aboot!**
I will struggle to jump over that hurdle because I am a little lame!

**That weeny lad has gor his claes aal clarty!**
That little boy has got extremely dirty clothes, he must have been playing in the mud!

**That owld lad with the big beak is deed canny!**
Although that old man has got a very big nose, he is still a really nice man to be acquainted with.

**His lass is geet bonny, ye knaa!**
His girlfriend is very pretty, I wish I could be acquainted with her!

**Will ye wisht!**
Could you please be quiet!

**She's a right charver, ye knaa!**
Did you know, that young girl is a little roguish!

**Wot are ye gawkin at?**
Why are you staring at me in that peculiar manner?

**When a gor in last nite, a hoyed up on the nettie!**
I had a too much alcohol last evening and consequently I was a little sick in the toilet.

### Divvent let ya dog pittle on me grass!

Your Labrador has urinated on my garden, please do not let it happen again, thank-you.

### That watta is scaadin!

The water in that tap is dangerously hot, be very careful!

### Aye, it is, aa knaa!

Yes, you are correct. The water is very hot: I have just scalded myself and it hurts!

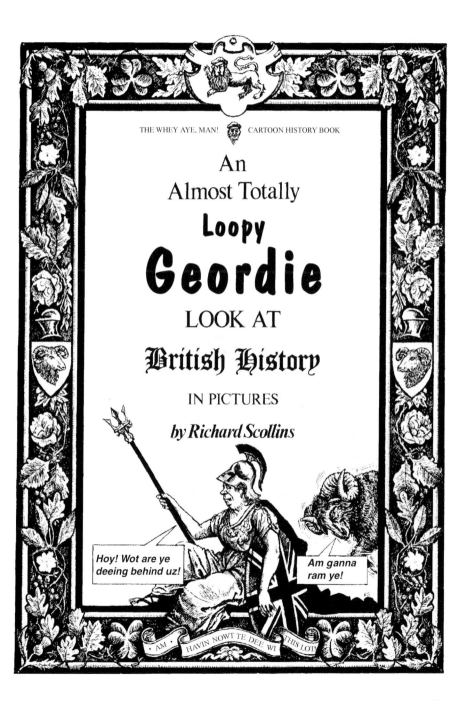

THE WHEY AYE, MAN! CARTOON HISTORY BOOK

# An
# Almost Totally
# Loopy
# Geordie
## LOOK AT
# British History
### IN PICTURES

*by Richard Scollins*

Hoy! Wot are ye deeing behind uz!

Am ganna ram ye!

·AM· HAVIN NOWT TE DEE WI THIS LOT

**Alfred and the Cakes — AD 878**

## Lady Godiva — AD 1057

**The Battle of Hastings — AD 1066**

# King John and Magna Carta — 1215

## The Battle of Agincourt — 1415

**Richard III at Bosworth — 1485**

**Henry VIII and Anne Boleyn — 1529**

**Raleigh and the Puddle — 1581**

**Francis Drake Goes Bowling — 1588**

## The First Night of 'Hamlet' — 1601

## The Gunpowder Plot — 1605

## The Execution of Charles I — 1649

## Charles II and Friends Hide From the Roundheads — 1651

## Bonnie Prince Charlie Arrives
## in Scotland — 1745

Nelson at Trafalgar — 1805

## Wellington Inspects His Troops — 1815

## The Charge of the Light Brigade — 1854

## Stanley Greets Dr. Livingstone — 1871

**Queen Victoria 'Not Amused' — 1878**

# THE END